Whispers In The Wind~A Collection Of Poems

Jennifer Sawatzky

BookLeaf Publishing

India | USA | UK

Presentation by *BookLeaf Publishing*

Web: www.bookleafpub.com

E-mail: info@bookleafpub.com

ISBN: 9789360940836

First edition 2024

For my children, my reasons, my muses my blessings~not a day goes by that you don't inspire me. I Love You all

For my love John B. for supporting me, finding me, loving me, always being patient & kind with my heart~

I Love you!

For my friends whom encouraged me to write thank you, I wouldn't have wrote this without your guidance and push!

~There is a difference between survival, existence, & truly living~

ACKNOWLEDGEMENT

To the Creator~Thank You
To The many whom has supported my dreams of writing and pushed me to continue writing and pushing forward to find a better path in life than the one I was on at one point~Thank You
To anyone who's ever believed in me, especially my grandma who told me I could do anything taught me to read and write. Thank you
To those whom told me it's ok to dream and that dreams can be achieved if only we work for them, Thank you.
To my love, my family, and my friends
Thank you for never giving up on me and always listening to my poems and writings, thank you for your patience.
Thank you to myself~for never giving up your dreams, for never loosing your passion for the little things that bring you pleasure in life even through the midst of chaos.

PREFACE

When confusion is present New Ideas are inseparable from the Spirits~

World void of Magic

I believe I was always a witch,
In a world sometimes void of magic…
Some days I felt lost,
Some days were just tragic!
Then time went on,
I found my own craft…
It was there all along,
Like a floating life raft!
Love entered fiercely,
Leading me again astray…
I remembered my power,
Suddenly found the way!
Way showers move brightly…
Like a star in the sky!
Circling around the earth,
Never fully understanding why!
I Am a solitary witch,
In a world sometimes void of magic…
Now using my sacred gifts,
Making each moment less tragic!

Love Like A Flower

Love grows slowly like a flower,
A seed in ones heart full of power!
Unknown the depth which a root reaches,
Or the strength in lessens that it teaches!
It takes imperfections in the weather,
To bind its cells an mesh together.
It breaks the ground and starts growing,
Heights it may reach no one is knowing.
It bends and turns but never breaks,
At times the growth may have it's aches!
Some days the unknown will leave you feeling
stressed,
Other times you will fall into love for comfort
and rest!
Love grows slowly like a flower,
It never fades like the sands in an hour…

Year of The Dragon

The Chinese New Year has begun,
Year of the dragon out comes the sun!
A year full of power prosperity luck,
Unchaining hearts that remain ever stuck!
Platters of fruit put out for spirits,
Prayers of thanks I hope they hear it!
Fruits of passion energy an love...
Given to ancestors in the stars above!
Vibrant bright colors clash and twirl,
like giants in the sky flying in a swirl!
Dragon's are fiery exuding emotion,
fierce and vast like the endless ocean!
They are making the way toward unity and
peace…
once the world wakes up and values their
release...
Fire an Ice can giveth or taketh away,
It will light the way to a glorious new day!

Love Equals Unity

Love an unity where the next pages turned,
Levels attained after the soul has been burned.
Places I found inspiration an love among
fellows,
While ever reaching those still caught in the
bellows.
Unity brings wholeness to one's Inner being,
New paths to life open senses to clearer seeing.
Good things happen to those who wait,
Be kind and forgiving, do not retaliate.
Things don't always need to make sense,
Life's troubles can make one's body tense.
Trust the process~learn to relax.
Feelings are feelings~not always facts.
The next chapters unwritten in ways yet
unlocking,
Love equals unity when darkness is unblocking.
Learning to let love within, writing new pages.
Music to those lost in life's waves of rages.

Whisper's In The Wind

Fire in the heart whisper in the winds,
Felt in the mind Is where it all begins.
You can hear the voices softly calling,
Even when life's trials can feel appalling.
We heal ourselves we heal one another,
Using Gifts earth given as she is our mother.
A giver of life and a maker of creation,
It spins in circles yet stays in one station.
Winds blow fast and rain loudly falls,
When listening quietly we hear the calls.
Whisper's in the wind that drive us ahead,
Ever stepping forward until this body is dead.
When the spirit's move on and leave human
sight,
Remember it is still there in the quiet of the
night.
Those whisper's may one day truly inspire,
for some they create mad burning desire!
Know which road you are on ever traveling fast,
Silent~listen…the whisper's will show us the
way at last.

Starseeds

Awakened with hypnotic stares here we are.
A new generation brought down from the stars.
We are more than mere human beings~
Into the souls of others we are seeing.
We came from stars near the Milky Way,
A distant place so strangely far away.
To make a change upon the ground.
Making moves silent without sound.
Powers in the eyes like hidden magic~
Protecting the land from all that's tragic.
Against all odds ~ we never fall down.
Lessons taught though the Heyoka clown.
Ones who teach both sacrifice and hope,
Before humanity tangles itself in the rope.
Sacred is the water to the sky beautifully blue,
Fighting with old fashioned love~unconditional
& true.

Family

Family is the thing that makes my heart skip a
beat!
It is everything meaningful even when I'm tired
& feel defeat.
They are there through all of life's special
seasons.
They love you for you and so many more
reasons.
Time spent together are precious little moments.
One common goal with many components.
There for each other through thick & through
thin.
Showing loving support whether we loose or we
win.
No one knows how many days are left of more
tomorrow's.
Tell them you love them now~time here is
borrowed.

The swallow

This small little bird ~ by the name of the swallow.
Nesting upon its home ~ far from empty or hollow.
There is a legend one whom stole from the sun,
So it is told how the fire once begun.
Carried so far upon soft graceful feathers...
To sustain life here through all different weathers.
Each year in remembrance we hang hollow gourd's,
For the gift of warmth deserves the greatest rewards!
Small creatures with abilities bigger than they appear.
Carrying knowledge to make our eyesight more clear.
Preservation and protection their communications bring.
Reminding us there is hidden wisdom in the words we sing.
Rise above the wind, do not be mundane.
See the world clearly do not go insane.
Strengthen and protect objectivity is key...
Gain some perspective look beyond the tree.

Clean your environment chase out the pest.
One day at a time comes all the rest.

The Foundation

The foundation of the home is broken and
cracked,
As the spirit was once where structure was
lacked.
Ripping holes into the house,
Spiders running even a mouse!
Pulling boards and rusty nails,
Filling the past into dusty pails!
Using the blood, sweat, and tears…
Clearing away the debris of fears.
When all is done, safe and sound the home will
be,
Inside its walls, live excitement, love, and
mystery.
When the foundation is solid it holds the
strength within,
Where life and new memories can again begin.

Spring Is Coming

Trees are budding flowers are waking,
Collecting sweet energy for the taking.
Spring is coming bright, swift, and soon,
Fish will be jumping at the call of the loon!
The nights becoming starlit an more active,
A warmth of the sun feeling so cute an
attractive!
Days are full of movement abruptly getting
longer,
The Smell of spring in the air helping us feel
ever stronger.
The moons ever shining it's light to guide,
Turning oceans swishing and swirling the tide.
Passionate about spring,
It's when I hear loudest nature sing!!

Farmer & The Plants

Planting their seeds,
getting ready for spring.
Love in the heart,
makes the energy sing!

The farmer and the plants,
birds, bees and ants...
Into the field again,
they do their little dance...

Then come the crops,
dancing with the dirt.
Growing each day,
fully alive and alert!

The farmer and the plants,
birds, bees, and ants...
Into the field again,
they do their little dance...

Building a future,
grown deep in the soil.
Engineers of hard work,
blood sweat and toil!

The farmer and the plants,
birds, bees and ants...
Into the field again,
they do their little dance...

A meeting of minds,
two thoughts becoming one.
Grown symbiotically,
with love earth and sun!

The farmer and the plants,
birds, bees and ants...
Into the field again,
they do their little dance...

It is said, watch closely enough they may even
put you into natures trance!!!
You, the farmer, and the plants,
Birds, bees, and ants…
Not the field WE do our little dance!!!

Today

Today is not yet over~
tomorrow is yet to come…
Webs we have weaved,
daily battles we have won.
A day late and a dollar short…
what we do to help hold down the fort!

Doors are meant to open,
tomorrow is yet to come~
Stairs are meant for stepping,
taking the elevator is dumb!

Take your time today~
In whatever deeds you do...
Enjoy the scenery,
And to yourself stay true!

Stay balanced an appreciate,
the moon stars and sun~
Never make light the battles,
you've courageously won!

Winds of Change

Today the wind was roughly blowing,
Buds on trees started swiftly growing.
The sun shining down ever bright,
Birds flying high as clouds out of sight.

Grass is green, alive, and has started showing.
Summers surprises in the earth slowly sewing.
Each new season brings new daily missions,
In each and every Creators conditions.

Animals awake stretching their bones,
Letting out rumbling roaring moans!
Bugs are about moving and shaking,
Some would say "mini earthquaking!"

Some stuck inside to their personal devil.
Yet in nature not even clouds are level!
Timeless days as clocks stop ticking,
cicada's wake up just to start clicking!

Running in cycles that we ALL do~
Ever to the heart & the earth stay true.
Today the wind was roughly blowing,
Life abounds for those of knowing!

~A Wild Woman~

A Wild woman deep in the dirt,
Is where she heals all the hurt.
Pouring love Into the ground,
The heartbeats solemn sound.
Helping plants to once again grow,
For the ones who used to care and know.

When a wild woman again is healed,
Much more to her is then revealed.
Revelations here are in the making,
After life's greedy little undertaking.
Forward stepping into the woods,
Where all is forgiven and understood.

As She grows older with the ages,
She gains the wisdom of the sages.
Life's lessons hit like waves of the sea,
The moons glow washes over her, you, and me.
Time stands still when she remembers her
power,
She soars with eagle higher than the highest
tower.

Passion of writing

Writing is one of my many passions,
Done so many ways & so many fashions.
The pen hits the paper thoughts start streaming,
Sometimes hard to know if I'm awake or
dreaming?
The roads I can traverse , the places I can go,
Endless possibilities of stories and characters I
know!
Words onto pages that travel through the ages.
Chapters of life's stages setting people free of
cages!
Sharing tales of love, family, and laughter!
Never knowing exactly what will come after!
Bleeding my thoughts and emotions into ink,
Releasing comparisons of what others think.
Part of writing is in the imaginations animations,
Thoughts to words ~ what beautiful creation's!
The passion of desire may come and go,
But the pen and paper is a friend I'll always
know!

Diamond in the rough

A diamond is created from the highest pressure
known to existence.
Two rocks coming together so hard there is no
longer resistance.
The results something so extremely hard it
cannot easily be broken.
During the hardest times REMEMBER the
words your soul has spoken.
YOU are a diamond in the making~a diamond in
the rough.
A tree standing tall with your roots in the ground
tough.
Time may take a toll upon your mind and deep
inside the soul.
You fear to much, scared your trust may burn
like coal.
Real eyes will wake up and grasp that you must
hold on tight,
for we all are to be given the ancient sight and
sacred light...
Inner-standing and Love in so many ways
Shining the light of life on all our days.

Cupids Arrows

Love is in the wind a blowing,
Cupid has the arrows going...
Listen closely you'll hear the whistle,
Just before it pokes you like a thistle!!!
Get ready for excitement stirred,
Like flying higher than a bird!!!
Love is blowing in the wind,
Duck quick or you'll get pinned!!!
Hearts of people set a glow,
Dancing til feet hurt…whoa!!!
Feisty love growing, feelings soaring,
Cupids job anything but boring!!!

Holding My Love

Feet on the ground head in the clouds,
Who knew we'd be where we are now?
Holding the love I've searched for my whole
life,
Wanting to be my husband~asking me to be his
wife…
One day we'll take that step after life's chaos has
settled,
When no longer our serenity and peace can be
meddled.
The time in between is where we grow most,
Sweet as a berries and fast as a ghosts!
To our needs an desires our hearts we shall
cater…
For every day with eachother is a gift from
Creator!

Crimes Against Humanity

Within peoples hearts their spirit's are cracking.
The crimes against humanity are ever stacking.
So many things done without consent or
consideration,
consequences wrought for future generations.
What we now leave behind will forever be an
impression,
To all whom follow every fateful succession.
Time to contemplate what is going on in this
world,
Before the beasts of destruction are forever
unfurled.
Burning material gains to ash~washing away all
greed,
No matter the money you earn or if you succeed.
The only thing that counts~the only thing that
matters,
 The world's heart breaks when the shell begins
to shatter!
The moves we make today~ the steps we take
tomorrow,
Are what fills the world with love instead of all
the sorrow.

Passion Flower

Passion flower so beautiful and sweet,
Slow to bloom like some people we meet!
None the less sweeter for the time they take,
Growing in the darkness at times must ache!
With patience, love, and a little light,
they bloom into Passion flowers out of sight.
So pretty they make you close your eyes to
blink,
Glancing again at the nature so colorful and
distinct!
Seasons of growth through the dirt in the
making,
Good for the soul straight from Creator for the
taking.
Colorful designs exuding like none other,
Gifts given swiftly from our Earth Mother.
Grown with passion in their roots,
No longer potted, mistreated, or mistook!

Writers Block

Thank you spirit for sharing your heart through
the pen,
So we don't ever have to feel alone here again...
None truly know the traumas we each have
survived,
We owe them nothing but our spirits on paper
revived!
Let go of anything trying to dim your beautiful
light,
It shines ever so brighter than the stars in the
night!
Lighting paths of inspiration for many like
myself~
To no longer feel dusty, broken, or wasted upon
a shelf~
Love, Blessings, Messages and Light
Thank you Inspiration my friend for all you set
right.
In times of laughter, tears, happiness, pain or
fright...
Through rays of sunshine, storms, even the dark
soul of the night...
Bits and pieces of the lives we bleed out through
the pen,

Just so we can live, laugh, and learn to BE
LOVE again!!!

www.ingramcontent.com/pod-product-compliance
Lightning Source LLC
LaVergne TN
LVHW010847200726
843508LV00012B/2792